Published simultaneously in 1995 by Exley Publications in Great Britain, and Exley
Giftbooks in the USA.

12 11 10 9 8 7 6 5 4 3

ISBN 1-85015-644-1

A HELEN EXLEY GIFTBOOK

Designed by Pinpoint Design Company.
Pictures researched by P. A. Goldberg and J. M. Clift, Image Select, London.
Typesetting by Delta, Watford.
Printed in China.
Exley Publications Ltd, 16 Chalk Hill, Watford, Herts WD1 4BN, United Kingdom.
Exley Giftbooks, 232 Madison Avenue, Suite 1206, NY 10016, USA.

Acknowledgements: The publishers are grateful for permission to reproduce copyright material. Whilst
every effort has been made to trace copyright holders, Exley Publications would be happy to hear from
any copyright holder not here acknowledged.
Picture Credits: Exley Publications is very grateful to the following individuals and organisations for
permission to reproduce their pictures: Archiv fur Kunst (AKG), Bridgeman Art Library (BAL), Edimedia
(EDM), Fine Art Photographic Library Ltd. (FAP), Giraudon (GIR), Scala (SCA). Front cover: © 1995
Maurice Chabas "Sunday", Waterhouse and Dodd, London/BAL; page 5: © 1995 Hugh Goldwyn
Riviere "The Garden of Eden", Guildhall Art Gallery, Corporation of London/BAL; page 6: AKG; page
8: Private Collection/BAL; page 11: EDM; page 12: Whitford and Hughes/BAL; page 15: SCA; page
17: © 1995 Chris Beetles; page 19: EDM; page 20: BAL; page 23: AKG; page 25: © 1995 Maria Dewey
Oakey "Garden in May", National Museum of American Art, Smithsonia/BAL; page 26: Magyar
Nemzeti Galeria, Budapest/BAL; page 29: AKG; page 31: 1995 Maurice Chabas "Sunday", Waterhouse
and Dodd, London/BAL; page 33: AKG; page 34: © 1995 Chris Beetles; page 37: 1995 George Hyde
Pownall "Theatre Time, Drury Lane, London", By courtesy of Bourne Gallery, Reigate/FAP; page 38:
Rijksmuseum Kroller-Muller, Otterloo/BAL; page 40: AKG; page 42: Musée des Augustins, Toulouse,
GIR/BAL; page 44: Hermitage, St. Petersburg/BAL; page 47: Victoria and Albert Museum,
London/BAL; page 48/9: AKG; page 50: Whitford and Hughes, London/BAL; page 53: AKG; page
54: © 1995 Patrick William Adam "Interior, Morning", Oldham Art Gallery, Lancs./BAL; page 57:
Chenil Galleries, London/BAL; page 58/9: AKG; page 60: © 1995 Chris Beetles.
Text credits: Conrad Aiken: "Music I Heard With You" from Collected Poems, 2nd edition, © 1953,
1970 by Conrad Aiken; renewed by Mary Aiken. Reprinted by permission of Oxford University Press,
Inc.; E. E. Cummings: "i like my body when it is with your body" and "my love" from Complete Poems
1904-1962, by E. E. Cummings, edited by George J. Firmage, by permission of W. W. Norton and Co.
Ltd. © 1925, 1976, 1991 by the Trustees for the E. E. Cummings Trust and George James Firmage, and
Liveright Publishing Corporation; Robert Frost: "Meeting and Passing" from "The Poetry of Robert
Frost" edited by Edward Connery Lathem, Jonathan Cape Ltd. Reprinted by permission of Random
House (UK) Ltd. on behalf of The Estate of Robert Frost and Henry Holt and Co.; Kahlil Gibran:
extract from "The Prophet" used by permission of The National Committee of Gibran 1951, © All rights
reserved; Heather Holden: "Summer Poem"; Elizabeth Jennings: "Winter Love" from Selected Poems,
Carcanet. Reprinted by permission of David Higham Associates Ltd; Katherine Mansfield: Extract from
letter to J. Middleton Murry. Reprinted by permission of The Society of Authors as the literary
representative of The Estate of Katherine Mansfield and Alfred Knopf Inc.; John Masefield: "An
Epilogue" from "Poems", William Heinemann Ltd. Reprinted by permission of The Society of Authors
as the literary representative of The Estate of John Masefield; Roger McGough: "our love will be an epic
film", © 1967, 1978 by Roger McGough from Summer With Monica, Whizzard/Andre Deutsch.
Reprinted by permission of the Peters, Fraser and Dunlop Group; Tom McGrath: "Reasons"; Peter
Roche: "Somewhere on the Way"; Edna St Vincent Millay: "Recuerdo" from Collected Poems, Harper
and Row, © 1922, 1950 by Edna St Vincent Millay. Reprinted by permission of Norma Millar Ellis;
Richard Sylvester: "Poem"; W. B. Yeats: "When You Are Old" from Collected Poems, Macmillan
Publishers Ltd. Reprinted by permission of Michael and Anne Yeats and A. P. Watt Ltd.; Yevgeny
Yevtushenko: "Colours" from Love Poems, Victor Gollancz Ltd., a division of Cassell.

A
TOKEN
of
LOVE

Love

POETRY

SELECTED BY

HELEN

EXLEY

EXLEY

NEW YORK • WATFORD UK

COLOURS

When your face
appeared over my crumpled life
at first I understood
only the poverty of what I have.
Then its particular light
on woods, on rivers, on the sea,
became my beginning in the coloured world
in which I had not yet had my beginning.
I am so frightened, I am so frightened,
of the unexpected sunrise finishing,
of revelations
and tears and the excitement finishing.
I don't fight it, my love is this fear,
I nourish it who can nourish nothing,
love's slipshod watchman.
Fear hems me in.
I am conscious that these minutes are short
and that the colours in my eyes will vanish
when your face sets.

YEVGENY YEVTUSHENKO

SUMMER POEM

I will bring you flowers
every morning for your breakfast
and you will kiss me
with flowers in your mouth
and you will bring me flowers
every morning when you wake
and look at me with flowers in your eyes

HEATHER HOLDEN

HOW DO I LOVE THEE?

How do I love thee? Let me count the ways.
I love thee to the depth and breadth and height
My soul can reach, when feeling out of sight
For the ends of Being and ideal Grace.
I love thee to the level of every day's
Most quiet need, by sun and candlelight.
I love thee freely, as men strive for Right;
I love thee purely, as they turn from Praise.
I love thee with the passion put to use
In my old griefs, and with my childhood's faith.
I love thee with a love I seemed to lose
With my lost saints – I love thee with the breath,
Smiles, tears, of all my life! – and, if God choose,
I shall but love thee better after death.

ELIZABETH
BARRETT
BROWNING

Love's philosophy

Over the mountains
    And over the waves;
Under the fountains,
    And under the graves;
Under floods that are deepest,
    Which Neptune obey;
Over rocks that are steepest,
    Love will find out the way.

You may train the eagle
    To stoop to your fist;
Or you may inveigle
    The phoenix of the east;
The lioness, ye may move her
    To give o'er her prey;
But you'll ne'er stop a lover:
    He will find out his way.

ANON

Our love will be an epic film
with dancing songs and laughter
the kind in which the lovers meet
and live happy ever after
our love will be a famous play
with lots of bedroom scenes
you are twenty-two you are monika
and only we know what that means

ROGER McGOUGH

SOMEWHERE ON THE WAY

I wanted to say a lot of things:
I wanted to say how often lately
Your bright image has wandered through
The dark rooms of my mind;
I wanted to say how good it is
To wake up every morning
Knowing that the day contains
Something that is you.

I wanted to say a lot of things:
I wanted to talk about
The changing colour of moments,
The silent secret language
Of bodies making love.
I wanted to say that you
Are always only as far from me
As thoughts are from thinking.

I wanted to say I love you
In fourteen foreign languages
But most of all (most
Difficult of all) in English.

I wanted to say a lot of things.
But they all seem to have lost themselves
Somewhere on the way. And now I'm here
There's nothing I can say except
Hello, and Yes, I'd like some coffee, and
What shall we find to talk about
Before the night burns out?

PETER ROCHE

This morning,
Beneath the cracks
In the kitchen ceiling,
Watched by the stains
On the walls
In spite of coffee
Spilled on the table cloth,
And burnt toast,
And broken promises,
In spite of
Many other reasons
Too numerous to mention,
And while a smashed chair
Looked on morosely,
You said you loved me.
Tonight
I shall fly to Rome
To have you declared
A bona fide
Miracle.

RICHARD SYLVESTER

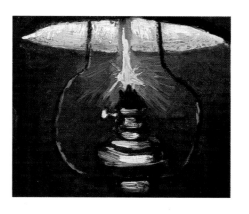

THE
HEART'S
FRIEND

Fair is the white star of twilight,
And the sky clearer
At the day's end;
But she is fairer, and she is dearer,
She, my heart's friend!

Fair is the white star of twilight,
And the moon roving
To the sky's end;
But she is fairer, better worth loving,
She, my heart's friend.

SHOSHONE LOVE SONG

MADRIGAL

My love in her attire doth show her wit,
   It doth so well become her;
For every season she hath dressings fit,
   For Winter, Spring, and Summer.
No beauty she doth miss
   When all her robes are on:
But Beauty's self she is
   When all her robes are gone.

ANON SEVENTEENTH CENTURY

TO HIS LOVE

Shall I compare thee to a summer's day?
Thou art more lovely and more temperate;
Rough winds do shake the darling buds of May,
And summer's lease hath all too short a date:
Sometimes too hot the eye of heaven shines,
And often is his gold complexion dimm'd;
And every fair from fair some time declines,
By chance, or nature's changing course, untrimm'd.
But thy eternal summer shall not fade
Nor lose possession of that fair thou ow'st;
Nor shall Death brag thou wand'rest in his shade
When in eternal lines to time thou grow'st.
So long as men can breathe, or eyes can see,
So long lives this, and this gives life to thee.

WILLIAM SHAKESPEARE

THE HILL

Breathless, we flung us on the windy hill,
　　Laughed in the sun, and kissed the lovely grass.
　　You said, 'Through glory and ecstasy we pass;
Wind, sun, and earth remain, the birds sing still,
When we are old, are old . . .' 'And when we die
　　All's over that is ours; and life burns on
Through other lovers, other lips,' said I,
　　'Heart of my heart, our heaven is now, is won!'

'We are Earth's best, that learnt her lesson here.
Life is our cry. We have kept the faith!' we said;
'We shall go down with unreluctant tread
Rose-crowned into the darkness!' . . .Proud we were,
And laughed, that had such brave true things to say.
– And then you suddenly cried, and turned away.

RUPERT BROOKE

I DO NOT LOVE THEE

I do not love thee! – no! I do not love thee!
And yet when thou art absent I am sad;
   And envy even the bright blue sky above thee,
Whose quiet stars may see thee and be glad.

I do not love thee! – yet, I know not why,
Whate'er thou dost seems still well done, to me:
   And often in my solitude I sigh
That those I do love are not more like thee!

I do not love thee! – yet, when thou art gone,
I hate the sound (though those who speak be dear)
   Which breaks the lingering echo of the tone
Thy voice of music leaves upon my ear.

I do not love thee! – yet thy speaking eyes,
With their deep, bright, and most expressive blue,
   Between me and the midnight heaven arise,
Oftener than any eyes I ever knew.

I know I do not love thee! yet, alas!
Others will scarcely trust my candid heart;
   And oft I catch them smiling as they pass,
Because they see me gazing where thou art.

CAROLINE ELIZABETH SARAH NORTON

I think the time has come, it really has come for us to do a little courting. Have we ever had time to stand under trees and tell our love? Or to sit down by the sea and make fragrant zones for each other? Do you know the peculiar exquisite scent of a tea-rose? Do you know how the bud opens – so unlike other roses and how deep red the thorns are and almost purple the leaves?

Wander with me 10 years – will you, darling? Ten years in the sun. It's not long – only 10 springs.

KATHERINE MANSFIELD, FROM LETTERS TO JOHN MIDDLETON MURRY

i like my body when it is with your
body.   It is so quite new a thing.
Muscles better and nerves more.
i like your body.   i like what it does,
i like its hows.   i like to feel the spine
of your body and its bones,and the trembling
-firm-smooth ness and which i will
again and again and again
kiss,   i like kissing this and that of you,
i like,slowly stroking the,shocking fuzz
of your electric fur,and what-is-it comes
over parting flesh....And eyes big love-crumbs,

and possibly i like the thrill

of under me you so quite new

E . E . C u m m i n g s

TO MARY

I sleep with thee and wake with thee,
    And yet thou art not there;
I fill my arms with thoughts of thee –
    And press the common air.
Thy eyes are gazing upon mine
    When thou art out of sight,
My lips are always touching thine
    At morning, noon, and night.

I think and speak of other things
    To keep my mind at rest,
But still to thee my memory clings
    Like love in woman's breast.
I hide it from the world's wide eye
    And think and speak contrary;
But soft the wind comes from the sky
    And whispers tales of Mary.

JOHN CLARE

A THUNDERSTORM IN TOWN

She wore a new "terra-cotta" dress,
And we stayed, because of the pelting storm,
Within the hansom's dry recess,
Though the horse had stopped; yea, motionless
We sat on, snug and warm.

Then the downpour ceased, to my sharp sad pain
And the glass that had screened our forms before
Flew up, and out she sprang to her door:
I should have kissed her if the rain
Had lasted a minute more.

THOMAS HARDY

RECUERDO

We were very tired, we were very merry –
We had gone back and forth all night on the ferry.
It was bare and bright, and smelled like a stable –
But we looked into a fire, we leaned across a table,
We lay on a hill-top underneath the moon;
And the whistles kept blowing, and the dawn came soon.

We were very tired, we were very merry –
We had gone back and forth all night on the ferry;
And you ate an apple, and I ate a pear,
From a dozen of each we had bought somewhere;
And the sky went wan, and the wind came cold,
And the sun rose dripping, a bucketful of gold.

We were very tired, we were very merry –
We had gone back and forth all night on the ferry.
We hailed, "Good-morrow, mother!" to a shawl-covered
    head,
And bought a morning paper, which neither of us read;
And she wept, "God bless you!" for the apples and the
    pears,
And we gave her all our money but our subway fares.

EDNA ST. VINCENT MILLAY

MEETING AND PASSING

As I went down the hill along the wall
There was a gate I had leaned at for the view
And had just turned from when I first saw you
As you came up the hill. We met. But all
We did that day was mingle great and small
Footprints in summer dust as if we drew
The figure of our being less than two
But more than one as yet. Your parasol
Pointed the decimal off with one deep thrust.
And all the time we talked you seemed to see
Something down there to smile at in the dust.
(Oh, it was without prejudice to me!)
Afterward I went past what you had passed
Before we met and you what I had passed.

ROBERT FROST

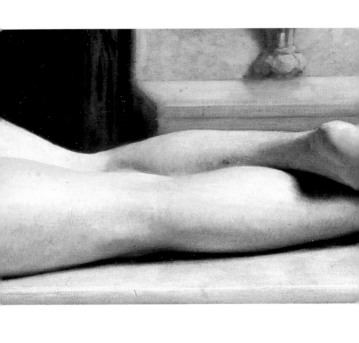

REASONS

Sweet one I love you
for your lovely shape,
for the art you make
in paint and bed and rhyme,
but most because we see
into each other's hearts,
there to read secrets
and to trust,
and cancel time.

TOM MCGRATH

ROMANCE

I will make you brooches and toys for your delight
Of bird-song at morning and star-shine at night.
I will make a palace, fit for you and me,
Of green days in forests, and blue days at sea.

I will make my kitchen, and you shall keep your room,
Where white flows the river and bright blows the broom,
And you shall wash your linen and keep your body white
In rainfall at morning and dewfall at night.

And this shall be for music when no one else is near,
The fine song for singing, the rare song to hear!
That only I remember, that only you admire,
Of the broad road that stretches and the roadside fire.

ROBERT LOUIS STEVENSON

Gladly I'll live in a poor mountain hut,

Spin, sew, and till the soil in any weather,

And wash in the cold mountain stream, if but

We dwell together.

ANON

my love
thy hair is one kingdom
   the king whereof is darkness
thy forehead is a flight of flowers

thy head is a quick forest
   filled with sleeping birds
thy breasts are swarms of white bees
   upon the bough of thy body
thy body to me is April
in whose armpits is the approach of spring

thy thighs are white horses yoked to a chariot
   of kings
they are the striking of a good minstrel
between them is always a pleasant song

my love
thy head is a casket
   of the cool jewel of thy mind
the hair of thy head is one warrior
   innocent of defeat
thy hair upon thy shoulders is an army
   with victory and with trumpets

thy legs are the trees of dreaming
whose fruit is the very eatage of forgetfulness

thy lips are satraps in scarlet
    in whose kiss is the combining of kings
thy wrists
are holy
    which are the keepers of the keys of thy blood
thy feet upon thy ankles are flowers in vases
    of silver

in thy beauty is the dilemma of flutes

    thy eyes are the betrayal
of bells comprehended through incense

E . E . C u m m i n g s

My tangled hair

I shall not cut:

Your hand, my dearest,

Touched it as a pillow.

ANON
JAPANESE VERSE

WHEN

YOU

ARE

OLD

When you are old and grey and full of sleep,
And nodding by the fire, take down this book,
And slowly read, and dream of the soft look
Your eyes had once, and of their shadows deep;

How many loved your moments of glad grace,
And loved your beauty with love false or true,
But one man loved the pilgrim soul in you,
And loved the sorrows of your changing face;

And bending down beside the glowing bars,
Murmur, a little sadly, how Love fled
And paced upon the mountains overhead
And hid his face amid a crowd of stars.

W. B. YEATS

MUSIC I HEARD WITH YOU

Music I heard with you was more than music,
And bread I broke with you was more than bread;
Now that I am without you, all is desolate;
All that was once so beautiful is dead.

Your hands once touched this table and this silver,
And I have seen your fingers hold this glass.
These things do not remember you, beloved, –
And yet your touch upon them will not pass.

For it was in my heart you moved among them,
And blessed them with your hands and with your eyes;
And in my heart they will remember always, –
They knew you once, O beàutiful and wise.

CONRAD AIKEN

INTER LOVE

Let us have winter loving that the heart
May be in peace and ready to partake
Of the slow pleasure spring would wish to hurry
Or that in summer harshly would awake,
And let us fall apart, O gladly weary,
The white skin shaken like a white snowflake.

ELIZABETH JENNINGS

When love beckons to you, follow him,
Though his ways are hard and steep.
And when his wings enfold you yield to him,
Though the sword hidden among his pinions
    may wound you.
And when he speaks to you believe in him,
Though his voice may shatter your dreams as the
    north wind lays waste the garden.

For even as love crowns you so shall he crucify
    you. Even as he is for your growth so is he for
    your pruning.
Even as he ascends to your height and caresses
    your tenderest branches that quiver in the
    sun,
So shall he descend to your roots and shake
    them in their clinging to the earth.
Like sheaves of corn he gathers you unto himself
He threshes you to make you naked.
He sifts you to free you from your husks.
He grinds you to whiteness.
He kneads you until you are pliant;
And then he assigns you to his sacred fire, that
    you may become sacred bread for God's
    sacred feast.

All these things shall love do unto you that you
    may know the secrets of your heart, and in
    that knowledge become a fragment of Life's
    heart.

But if in your fear you would seek only love's
   peace and love's pleasure,
Then it is better for you that you cover your
   nakedness and pass out of love's threshing-
   floor,
Into the seasonless world where you shall laugh,
   but not all of your laughter, and weep, but
   not all of your tears.

Love has no other desire but to fulfil itself.
But if you love and must needs have desires, let
   these be your desires:
To melt and be like a running brook that sings
   its melody to the night.
To know the pain of too much tenderness.
To be wounded by your own understanding of
   love;
And to bleed willingly and joyfully.
To wake at dawn with a winged heart and give
   thanks for another day of loving;
To rest at the noon hour and meditate love's
   ecstasy;
To return home at eventide with gratitude;
And then to sleep with a prayer for the beloved
   in your heart and a song of praise upon your
   lips.

KAHLIL GIBRAN,

FROM *THE PROPHET*

L O V E

So the year's done with!
   (Love me for ever!)
All March begun with,
   April's endeavour;
May-wreaths that bound me
   June needs must sever;
Now snows fall round me,
Quenching June's fever –
   (Love me for ever!)

ROBERT BROWNING